COUNTERATTACK

COUNTERATTACK

Montgomery and the Battle of the Bulge

The hidden story of Field Marshal Montgomery
and the British led victory over Hitler's last great gamble.

Robert Oulds

© Robert Oulds 2022

Robert Oulds has asserted his rights under the Copyright, Design and Patents Act, 1988, to be identified as the author of this work.

First published in 2022 by Sharpe Books.
This edition published in 2022 by The Bruges Group.

Synopsis

16TH DECEMBER 1944, western Europe. Hitler launches his last great gamble in the west. Fanatical Nazi soldiers were unleashed on unsuspecting Americans resting far away from where they thought the fighting would take place. The Battle of the Bulge was underway.

American commanders, earlier that fateful morning, thought the Germans were as good as beaten. British commander Bernard Law Montgomery knew otherwise. The famous Field Marshal had months before raised the alarm, telling the Supreme Allied Commander, General Eisenhower, of the threat. Monty's warnings were not heeded, and tens of thousands of American soldiers paid the ultimate price.

Shocked and nearly overawed Americans were pushed aside as Hitler's panzers raced towards Montgomery's forces in Belgium. Despite the many Allied disagreements and jealous intriguing from some American commanders, Monty, as he was affectionately known, calmly halted and then drove back what was a ferocious assault. Yet, because of this success his reputation was besmirched by those who could not accept his leading role in the fight. Attempts were made to write his contribution out of history.

This is the previously untold and until now hidden story of Field Marshal Montgomery and his British led victory over Hitler's ruthless counteroffensive. This epic confrontation that we know today as the Battle of the Bulge.

In this book the military historian Robert Oulds looks at the key role that the controversial victor of El-Alamein played in defeating Adolf Hitler's bold surprise attack.

The events of this great conflict are explained to the reader as are the tactics, weapons, armies, the key commanders, and the strategy that Montgomery used to thwart Hitler's plans. Robert Oulds also busts some long-held Hollywood myths and looks at the enormous controversy surrounding Montgomery.

Now it is time to tell the long overdue story of Montgomery and the Battle of the Bulge.

"The operations of the American 1st Army had developed into a series of individual holding actions. Montgomery's contribution to restoring the situation was that he turned a series of isolated actions into a coherent battle fought according to a clear and definite plan. It was his refusal to engage in premature and piecemeal counter-attacks which enabled the Americans to gather their reserves and frustrate the German attempts to extend their breakthrough."

The German commander of the 5th Panzer Army,
General Hasso von Manteuffel,
commenting on Montgomery's role in
the Battle of the Bulge

Contents

Introduction 11

The Allied Commanders 13

The Axis Commanders 15

The Opposing Armies 16

The Axis Weapons 18

The Allied Weapons 20

The Battlefield 22

Prelude to the Battle 23

Hitler's strategy 26

The Battle 31

The Allies at war: The Infamous Press Conference 46

Aftermath 49

Why the Allies Won 53

Appraising the myths of the Battle of the Bulge 56

Timeline: The Battle of the Bulge at a Glance 59

About the Author 63

Endnotes 65

Introduction

ON THE MORNING of 16th December 1944 Field Marshal Montgomery, known affectionately as Monty by his men in the 21st Army Group, his countrymen, and colleagues, was playing golf. In search of light relief, he had flown to Eindhoven, landing on a fairway. Monty had arranged to meet the professional golf player Dai Rees. Almost as soon as they had begun their game, Montgomery received a scratchy report of a major German assault on the US First Army. Although this army was not under Montgomery's command, he, unlike Drake, did not stay to finish his game. Instead, he flew back to his tactical HQ in Zonhoven from where he could take action.

At the same time General Dwight Eisenhower, the Supreme Allied Commander in Europe, was hosting the commander of the American 12th Army Group, General Omar Bradley, in the Trianon Palace Hotel, in the historic city of Versailles near Paris. They met to discuss the severe shortages of soldiers which Allied infantry divisions were suffering from, however, events were to overtake their discussions. Upon receiving reports on the unfolding fighting, Eisenhower and Bradley, like Montgomery, recognised the seriousness of the situation. Together over a bottle of champagne and a game of bridge, the two American generals considered their response to this new German blitzkrieg.

The Battle of the Bulge was seen as a battle between Nazi Germany and its American opponent. In terms of the enormous amount of lives lost this is true but history has largely overlooked the important role that the British Field Marshal, Bernard Law Montgomery, played in this epic and deadly struggle. That is, until now.

Despite Monty's contribution being decisive even he, a renowned self-publicist, was reluctant to talk about it after the Second World War. In his memoirs he wrote, *'I think the less one says about this battle the better, for I fancy that whatever I do say will almost certainly be resented.'*

Such was the bitterness caused by Eisenhower handing over two armies formerly commanded by the US General Omar Bradley to Montgomery's leadership and the anger over misreported and misunderstood comments made by the British Field Marshal that some historians have sought to almost write him out of the fighting altogether. Now it is time to tell the long overdue story of Montgomery and the Battle of the Bulge. Monty's role in stopping Germany's last great attack in the west led to American commanders sniping at him. Britain's most famous, and, as public celebrations after the war have shown, most popular World War Two commander also had to contend with attacks and subterfuge from the Nazis.

During the fighting, an attack from the Luftwaffe in support of the German ground offensive destroyed Montgomery's personal transport plane, which had been gifted to him by General Eisenhower for the duration of the war. There were also rumours of German assignation squads that had been sent out to kill the British Field Marshal. One way or the other Monty was in the firing line and the Battle of the Bulge was very much his battle. What is more, the forces that were placed under Montgomery's control faced the main thrust of the German onslaught.

This was a battle of epic proportions, and it received its name from the British Prime Minister Winston Churchill. To some it is known as the Ardennes Offensive, but its most well-known name derives from the massive indent - or bulge - in the American lines that was created by the Germans driving the US army back.

The Battle of the Bulge personifies the personalities and individual style of leadership of the three main characters that were at the heart of this great fight: Montgomery, Hitler, and Eisenhower.

The Allied Commanders

FIELD MARSHAL BERNARD Law Montgomery, Monty, was the British hero of the Second Battle of El-Alamein who had then chased Rommel back across much of North Africa. Churchill said of this battle that 'Before Alamein we never had a victory. After Alamein we never had a defeat.' Monty then commanded the Eighth Army during its invasion of Sicily and mainland Italy. Prior to preparing for the D-Day landings and the Normandy campaign, in which he was the commander of all ground forces he had breached the Gustav Line in Italy. Montgomery respected the importance of the individual soldier. His style of leadership concentrated on making sure that all his subordinates from army commanders down to the individual soldier, or munitions worker in a factory, knew what their role was, why it was important, and what was expected of them. He would habitually visit the troops to explain his plans and raise their morale. He did not believe in wasting lives in attacks unless his armies were sufficiently prepared to deliver victory. Montgomery's leadership during the Battle of Bulge was classic Monty in action.

General Dwight D Eisenhower was the Supreme Commander of Allied Forces in Europe. He had overseen the command structure behind the November 1942 Allied landing in North Africa and the driving out of German forces from that continent, Sicily, much of Italy and, up until the Battle of the Bulge, most of France. His was an enormous burden. Despite never seeing combat before he entered World War II, General Eisenhower was popular and widely respected for his diplomatic skills, these would be severely tested during the Battle of the Bulge. His cautiousness and repeated attempts to keep his bickering subordinate generals happy meant that no one commander received a plethora of supplies. Nor did Eisenhower significantly prioritise one commander's operations over another's. This led to the so-called Broad Front Strategy. Arguably, this created the circumstances that made the Battle of the Bulge possible. Under Eisenhower's instructions the Allies fanned out towards the Rhine, dispersing rather than concentrating their force.

General Omar Bradley was the commander of the 12th Army Group. This powerful collection of armies was in the direct path of the German attack. Serving directly under him at the start of the conflict were Generals Courtney Hicks Hodges who commanded the First Army, William Hood Simpson who commanded the Ninth Army, and George Patton who commanded the Third Army. He had been Bradley's superior prior to an incident where he abused some American soldiers who were in hospital with acute combat stress after fighting in Sicily. He also confronted medical personnel treating the shell-shocked soldiers.

The Axis Commanders

ADOLF HITLER, THE leader of Nazi Germany, was a gambler who took impulsive, reckless, and desperate military decisions throughout the Second World War. No other operation typifies this trait better than the Battle of the Bulge. Yet, even for Hitler there was a degree of logic at work. He held the belief in the *endsieg*, the final victory, so kept on fighting when in reality all was lost. In his relatively simplistic view, all that was needed to secure a positive outcome was to keep fighting, take the offensive, and, through sheer strength of will, Germany would be triumphant.

Field Marshal Gerd von Rundstedt, after being re-appointed to the overall command of German forces in the west, had managed to stabilise the front. He was then given the unwelcome task of planning the details of Hitler's Ardennes Counteroffensive. von Rundstedt was conservative both in terms of his background, he was the quintessential Prussian officer, and militarily, for he was risk averse. Yet this operation was abundant with jeopardy.

The impulsive Field Marshal Walter Model, known as Hitler's Fireman, served under von Rundstedt but had direct operational control over the three armies that took part in Hitler's attack. General Sepp Dietrich, commanded the Sixth Panzer Army, General Hasso von Manteuffel, commander the Fifth Panzer Army and General Adolf Robert Erich Brandenberger, commanded the Seventh Army.

The Opposing Armies

THE FORCE WHICH Hitler put into the field was a major one and consisted of a total of twenty-four divisions, ten of which were panzer and panzer grenadier divisions. These were in three armies: the Fifth Panzer Army, the Sixth Panzer Army, and the Seventh Army. At the start of the fighting there were 200,000 German men-at-arms and at the height of the engagement, the Reich fielded half-a-million men in this great struggle.

Both the Fifth and the Sixth Panzer Armies contained elite and well-equipped armoured *Waffen*-SS (armed SS) units; this was the military wing of the Nazi Party. Its soldiers were highly motivated and believed in the cause of National Socialism. However, the Seventh Army was an understrength formation. It was primarily made up of infantry from the regular German army known as the *Heer*. One such unit was called the Stomach Division because it consisted of those who were ill with abdominal sickness, but just well enough to fight, or at least become cannon fodder. They had to be segregated from their colleagues in other divisions in order not to spread disease.

Despite the Seventh Army's problems, the building up of such a massive strategic reserve and the supplying of tanks to the Fifth and Sixth armies was a major accomplishment especially after the severe losses which occurred during the fighting in France earlier in the summer of 1944. Eisenhower, also known fondly as Ike, did not believe that such a powerful force would be ready to attack the Allies in the winter that year. Recklessly, however, German troops were moved from the Vistula Front facing the might of the Red Army to take part in the Battle of the Bulge.

The American forces in the firing line were in the First Army and the Ninth Army. To the north of those formations was Monty's 21st Army Group. It consisted of two field armies: the Canadian First Army and the British Second Army. Armoured divisions from the British Army joined the fighting in the Battle of the Bulge. The Third Army, which entered the fight against the Seventh Army, was commanded by General George Patton.

At the start of the Battle of the Bulge the Germans achieved local superiority against their American adversaries. They outnumbered them by more than two-to-one, and as their initial US opponents were lightly armed divisions resting from the front, the Germans therefore used superior weaponry. As reinforcements were brought into action, the Allied forces became more numerous than the Germans and outstripped their army by more than 100,000 troops. In time they could also bring better weapons to bear than those at the disposal of the Nazi belligerents.

The Axis Weapons

THE BATTLE OF the Bulge saw the deployment of some of Nazi Germany's most effective armaments. These were the Panzer IV tank, which was especially effective when it was upgraded to a 75mm high-velocity gun. This was the most numerous German tank type in the Battle of the Bulge. Also used in the Ardennes offensive were 400 Panthers, which shared the 75mm gun, and when judged individually was arguably one of the best medium tanks of the war and the heavy Tiger tank using the famed 88mm gun and the panzer's further overdeveloped version the Tiger II, also known as the King Tiger, a monstrous beast that dwarfed its namesake. The Tiger variants were powerful and excellently armoured. However, their fuel efficiency, especially in the case of the Tiger II, and their reliability, was poor at best and often woeful. Due to its excessive weight, the King Tiger also had difficulty crossing some bridges but when in open country they were more than a match for Allied tanks, however the Nazis could only field little more than 100 Tigers. However, added to their arsenal were; artillery, self-propelled guns, and tank destroyers such as the *Jagdpanzer* IV.

The German soldier could also employ the *panzerfaust* (tank or armour fist) which was a numerous and cheap disposable anti-tank weapon which was effective at short distances and the *panzerschreck* (tank fright or armour fright). This 88mm rocket propelled grenade could penetrate the defences of all Allied tanks and had a range of up to 150 metres.

The German soldiers were also equipped with rifles and their own effective and reliable submachine guns. Some also used the *Sturmgewehr* 44. This translates into English as 'assault rifle' and it is from here that this genre of weapons and their name derives. This gun was to form the basis for the still in use today Russian AK-47 and its derivatives; which had recently been claiming Allied lives from Iraq to Afghanistan. Amongst the most terrifying weapons used in the Battle of the Bulge was the MG42 belt fed general purpose machine gun. This weapon could smother an area with bullets being fired at the enormous rate of more than 1,200 rounds per minute. Its unique sound and fast withering fire, deadly at over 1,000 yards, led to the American soldiers nicknaming the weapon 'Hitler's buzzsaw'.

The Luftwaffe employed a flak corps, made available to provide anti-aircraft artillery to defend the soldiers on the ground against attack from above. The Nazi war planes used during the Battle of the Bulge consisted of the Messerschmitt Bf 109 and the Focke-Wulf Fw 190. They were both single engine piston driven fighter planes. The Bf 109 was still an effective weapon of war but after nearly a decade of service in the Luftwaffe other models were beginning to surpass it. By the time of the Battle of the Bulge the Focke-Wulf Fw 190 was the main tool in the Luftwaffe's fighter force, known in German as the *Jagdwaffe*. This plane effectively operated on parity with the best planes that the Allies had at their disposal. However, the Luftwaffe had lost many of its most talented and best trained pilots.

The Allied Weapons

THE ROYAL AIR Force, the Royal Canadian Air Force and the United States Army Air Forces were far superior in number and, at this time in the war, skill. The Allies possessed superb ground-attack aircraft, namely the Mosquito, Typhoon, and Thunderbolt. The well armoured P-47 Thunderbolt with its eight .50 calibre Browning machine guns was also a superb fighter plane and an excellent complement to the P-51D Mustang, and Supermarine Spitfire. The Allies could also rely upon resupply from the air, in particular the Douglas C-47 Skytrain, also known as the Dakota. This transport plane was to prove decisive in the fighting for the soon to be encircled town of Bastogne. It parachuted in supplies to the besieged 101st Airborne Division enabling them to stop the Germans from capturing the invested town.

On the ground, whilst the Germans had the individually superior Panther, Tiger, and Tiger II tanks, as well as the Panzer IV which operated on near parity with late war Allied tanks, the western Allies could count on the far higher number of M4 Sherman medium tanks and the British variant Sherman Firefly mounting the powerful 17 pounder gun. To give the Allies extra firepower the Americans had the M18 Hellcat tank destroyer. This offered little in the way of armoured protection but its powerful 76mm gun packed a deadly punch. US infantrymen also used the M9 rocket-propelled grenade launcher, commonly called the 'Bazooka'. This enabled otherwise lightly armed troops to resist German tanks and prevent them from overrunning Allied lines. This handheld shoulder mounted cannon was far superior to the British spring loaded PIAT anti-tank weapon. The Americans soldiers also used artillery to target and destroy the German panzers.

The American infantry man was well armed. Some were equipped with the reliable and easy to use M3 submachine gun, known to the GI's as the 'Grease Gun'. This fired the .45 calibre round and was effective at close range. US soldiers could also rely upon the highly successful M1 Garand semi-automatic rifle. This .30 calibre gun was a battle winning weapon. The Americans could also depend upon the heavy and rapid firepower of the Browning M1919 machine gun, which similarly fired the .30 calibre round in quick succession; and the .50 calibre 'Ma Deuce' M2 heavy machine gun. Both these effective belt fed machine guns are still in use to this day, more than a century after they were originally introduced.

British soldiers could bring into combat the reliable .303 Lee Enfield bolt-action rifle. Despite the drawback of the requirement to chamber each round using a small handle an experienced marksman could fire 30 aimed shots per minute. Slow by today's standards but it was the British army's tradition that soldiers should not waste their ammunition. To strengthen a British platoon a soldier in that unit possessed the Bren Gun. This automatic machine gun also fired the powerful .303 round. This highly accurate weapon is arguably one of the finest light machine guns ever produced and was in service with the British army from 1938 until as late as 1991; with it seeing action in all wars including the Falklands and the First Gulf War. British forces also possessed a submachine gun known as the Sten gun. This fired the 9mm parabellum round and, like the American Grease Gun, it was effective at close range. The Sten was not always reliable but as it was cheap to produce it was thus very economic.

The Battlefield

THE ARDENNES, A rugged area mainly in the part of Belgium that is close to the border with Luxembourg, was being used by Generals Eisenhower and Bradley to rest weary detachments. Those commanders felt that it was unlikely that an attack would be made across this region as it had poor road links and was far from hospitable terrain. It is a hilly area that in parts is deeply forested. The Ardennes region is also dissected by many rivers and contains a number of ridges. There were also settlements that could be tuned into bastions capable of holding out against the German advance.

The topography of the Ardennes made its climatic conditions unpredictable and severe. Both sides had to fight against a common enemy, the weather; but it affected the two sides in different ways. The winter of 1944/45 was one of the coldest in living memory; at the start of the battle the meteorological circumstances were both a benefit and a curse to the Germans. At the beginning of the fighting the ground was muddy, which restricted the mobility of the heavy German armour and slowed their advance. The environment that makes precipitation common in the Ardennes conversely gave the Germans the advantage that the low-lying cloud grounded Allied aircraft, thus at the beginning of the Battle of the Bulge one of the main strengths which the allies possessed, air superiority, was neutered. The weather conditions change often and the contrast between the undulating and rugged topography alter the balance of power in as dramatic a fashion as the extremes of the climate and the lay of the land which added to inclement weather. The cold which followed the fog lifting actually hardened the ground thus aiding the heavy German tanks, making life very difficult for the American soldiers, many of whom did not receive adequate winter clothing.

Prelude to the Battle

THE BREAKOUT FROM Normandy and the subsequent dash across France into Belgium, taking the Allies close to the borders of Germany, had been a magnificent victory. However, this alternative version of Blitzkrieg began to break down.

After the success of the summer of 1944 the autumn proved to be a difficult time for the Allies. Eisenhower had failed to prioritise the capture of the key port of Antwerp from where supplies could be brought in; instead, he urged the Anglo-American forces to push on towards the Rhine. At the same time none of the numerous Allied armies were not given enough adequate resources to guarantee success. Montgomery's northern thrust had only received part of the support that he wanted, resulting in the ill-fated Operation Market Garden. At the same time, Patton's advance had run out of steam before the German border. Eisenhower's stratagem was simplistic '*advance to the Rhine*' and '*kill Germans*'. Whilst there was merit in killing Germans, this approach to warfare was far from profound. Eisenhower's so-called Broad Front Strategy led to Allied strength being dissipated as he sent his forces off in diverging, instead of converging, directions. What is more they were still a long way from achieving the objectives set by Eisenhower on 28th October 1944, namely the capture of the Ruhr and the Saar; two areas that were vital to the Nazi armament industry.

Eisenhower was a skilled diplomat who also possessed great organisational abilities, yet he had never seen combat. Clearly, he had not sufficiently studied the German experience in North Africa. Nor what occurred on the Eastern Front where the Wehrmacht became overstretched on the Steppe; and where the Red Army had recklessly advanced on a broad front after their victory outside Moscow. The renowned Prussian Soldier and Military Philosopher, Carl von Clausewitz, had also warned that unrestrained success can lead to an army becoming overextended, undermining its own logistical base, from where the enemy can extinguish its undersupplied and isolated opponent.

Montgomery was becoming concerned about the increasing number of US casualties, which were causing a shortage of manpower in Bradley's 12th Army Group which similarly suffered supply problems such as a shortage of ammunition. Due to resources being split between the different unconnected thrusts, the western Allies had not been able to breach or bypass the fixed German defences called the Westwall, also known as the Siegfried Line, which guarded the Fatherland. Worse still, an enormous weakness had opened up in US lines.

Montgomery's predominantly British and Canadian forces in his 21st Army Group were in a strong position and represented a powerful and cohesive front. Yet further south US forces were positioned with a gap of around 100 miles in their defences which covered the Ardennes, an area which was held by a corps of just four weak resting divisions. They were not ready for combat against the mighty host that was soon to bear down on them. This was the weakest part of the American line, and the German blow was scheduled to fall right on it; cutting General Omar Bradley's 12th Army Group in half. On 28th November 1944 Montgomery had warned Eisenhower about this, suggesting that Patton's Third Army should be moved north to not only fill the gap, but also to engage and destroy the Sixth Panzer Army, the most powerful Axis mobile force in the country, the failure to heed that advice was to have grave consequences.

The Supreme Allied Commander, General Eisenhower, and General Bradley had effectively split the 12th Army Group in two, dispersing its strength on multiple axes. Each part of it was deployed to attack different locations in offensives that were not mutually supportive. In the north the US First Army was based around the historic city of Aachen. They were beginning an operation on 13th December against the Roer dams but much of the offensive capability of this thrust was delayed by atrocious weather. In the south the US Third Army was due to attack the strategically significant Saar region of Germany which is rich with coal deposits. In between was the vulnerable Ardennes.

After the Second World War Eisenhower was open about the tactical failings that allowed the Germans to seize the initiative. He wrote:

'*The responsibility for maintaining only four divisions on the Ardennes front and for running the risk of a large German penetration in that area was mine… This plan gave the Germans opportunity to launch his attack against a weak portion of our lines.'*

Eisenhower, in agreement with Bradley, instead of waiting for reinforcements was pushing the attacks *'to the extreme limit of our ability, and it was this decision that was responsible for the startling successes of the first week of the German December attacks.'* And no doubt the enormous casualties.

Eisenhower had seen that this weakness in the front existed but after his deliberations with Bradley he concluded that the threat, if an attack did occur, could be eliminated without great risk. In addition to these suspicions Eisenhower received alarming intelligence reports. Not only had they lost sight of the new formation that was the Sixth Panzer Army but at the same time there was increasing concern about a German build up opposite the Americans in the Ardennes.1 Despite all this the storm that was to break on this new front was to shock the American forces who were nearly overawed by the ferocious assault.

As the Allied advance first stalled and then ground to a halt, Hitler was given the opportunity to not only re-establish a secure front in the west from where resistance could be organised to deliver counterattacks, but he also had the opportunity to build up a strategic reserve to deliver these blows. To this end the Nazis increased their divisions facing the western Allies from just 23 to seventy. What is more the Germans now had available the latest equipment. The American's were to pay dearly for handing the initiative back to Hitler.

Hitler's strategy

'History repeats itself, first as tragedy, then as farce.'

IN LATE 1944 Hitler was a desperate man. On all fronts German forces had been driven back and the Fatherland was being pounded from the air day and night by heavy strategic bombers. The Nazi dream of survival, let alone conquest, needed a miracle. It is therefore perhaps not surprising that Hitler in 1944 settled on a similar strategy to save his thousand-year Reich that had earlier won him a great victory over Britain and France in 1940. This was an offensive that ultimately isolated the British Expeditionary Force from many of their French partners and it started with a surprise attack coming through the seemingly impenetrable forest of the Ardennes. What's more, the commander of both the 1940 and the 1944 drives across this region was none other than Field Marshal Gerd von Rundstedt.

Whereas von Rundstedt favoured a limited offensive, Hitler who was the driving force behind the attack, had other plans and wanted an all-out operation. Other generals shared von Rundstedt's view and instead of using the massive resources used in the Battle of the Bulge against the west, they wanted the strength of these armies to be employed on the eastern front against the Russians. Hitler, however, wanted to defeat the allies in the west first allowing for a full concentration against the Red Army later. Yet after the July 1944 bomb plot against the Führer and the resulting purges, the German generals were unwilling to oppose his plans. The Ardennes Offensive had three main prongs to its attack. The Sixth Panzer Army had the main objective of striking north-west directly towards Antwerp which it was tasked with capturing. The city of Liège was also in its path. The Fifth Panzer Army was in the middle of the prongs. This had the aim of capturing Brussels. The third thrust, consisting of the Seventh Army, was primarily an infantry attack with little armoured strength. It was directly to the west and had the aim of tying up American forces and covering the south. The Seventh Army formed the southern shoulder, or flank, of the bulge. Montgomery faced those forces that were attacking on the northern side towards Brussels and Antwerp.

This plan was organised in the utmost secrecy and was codenamed Operation Watch on the Rhine (*Wacht am Rhein*). It was named after a German patriotic song, whose name also gave the impression of an innocuous defensive campaign. The operation was to be launched as soon as the weather conditions deteriorated to such a degree that low lying cloud and heavy fog would ground the overwhelmingly superior Allied air forces. This was such a key factor that the German breakthrough had to be decisive before the skies cleared and Anglo-American air power could be brought to bear on the Germans below.

The plan also included English speaking Germans operating behind Allied lines to sow confusion, disrupt communications and capture vital bridges over the river Meuse in advance of the main armoured units. This plan was created by Hitler and was under the leadership of the famed Nazi Commando Otto Skorzeny, the man who led the rescue of Mussolini, liberating the man once known as *Il Duce* from Italian captivity. The scheme was codenamed Operation *Grief* and it involved German paratroopers disguised as British and American soldiers. It was hoped that because they were to take off their guises and wear German uniforms if engaged in combat, they would therefore escape the firing squad if captured. To be taking part in a battle whilst not in uniform and even worse posing as one's opponents would put them beyond the rules of war allowing them to be treated as spies and illegal combatants. As such they were not entitled to the protections then laid down in the Geneva Convention.

It was not uncommon for a near defeated enemy to try one last gamble and Hitler was a degenerate gambler. In March 1918 the German Empire attempted to snatch victory from the jaws of defeat in a last desperate thrust known as the Spring Offensive or *Kaiserschlacht* (Kaiser's Battle). This offensive, planned by General Ludendorff, like the Battle of Bulge sought to destroy the British Army in France which would then force the French to agree to an armistice. This attack and its supporting operations eventually failed to break the entente but not before it inflicted enormous casualties and spread panic amongst the Allied leadership. The thinking behind the Battle of the Bulge was therefore quite unoriginal but it still caught the Americans off guard.

The western Allies, despite their own problems of supply and manpower, had an enormous advantage in both men and material. To the Nazis it seemed like they had an almost inexhaustible supply which were streaming in via the port of Antwerp. On 4th September 1944 Monty's 21st Army Group had captured the key port of Antwerp. This port had become a vital hub for bringing supplies to the Allied armies. This build up had to be stopped.

It was intended to not only cut off this flow at the source, Antwerp, but also to capture the supply centres of Liège and Brussels. This would not only deprive the Allies of their resources but would also power the German drive towards Antwerp. Nazi success, in fact, depended upon it. Germany was suffering from a severe shortage of fuel and could not supply its thirsty panzers with enough to sustain the *Heer*, the German Army, and their *Waffen*-SS Nazi co-belligerents, in combat. Since the great port's loss, Hitler, who fully understood its strategic significance, had been trying to render it unusable. On Hitler's orders the Scheldt Estuary, which governed the approach by sea to Antwerp, was stubbornly defended but eventually cleared by the Canadian Army, with British support, and eventually the mines in the harbour would come to be removed. Yet, Hitler still did not give up. Without success Hitler fired more than half the V2 rockets at his disposal at Antwerp in an attempt to destroy the dock facilities. Now he tasked the German forces in the Battle of the Bulge to capture the city and its harbour.

The other main strategic aim of the operation that we know as the Battle of the Bulge was not to capture territory held by US forces but those under the control of Field Marshal Montgomery whose troops Hitler hoped to isolate and destroy. Hitler envisioned that the main thrusts aimed through the Ardennes would advance as far as the British held port of Antwerp in Belgium thus isolating the British and the Canadians from the Americans. Capturing Antwerp would cut-off Montgomery's 21st Army Group from other Allied formations. Hitler fantasised that this would allow the British to be destroyed. Or at the least he anticipated that this would shatter the military and political unity between the forces of the British Empire and her American progeny.

Hitler was a man that looked to the past. He knew that the Prussian King, Frederick the Great, had been saved from almost certain defeat when divisions emerged between his enemies. Perhaps the Fuhrer would have the same fortune. Hitler hoped that by achieving the tactical victory of dividing the Anglo-American forces militarily and geographically, with the British to the North and the Americans to the South, he would achieve a strategic success in the western theatre of operations. Hitler imagined that this would result in a political split that could potentially end the western Allies' war against his Nazis regime.

Hitler had made a great mistake by starting a war on multiple fronts. However, the Italian Front had been stabilised after Eisenhower diverted resources from that campaign to Operation Dragoon; the Gallic-American landings in southern France. The Führer also had trust in German wonder-weapons, known as *Wunderwaffe*, such as jet and rocket planes. He expected that they would stabilise the air war which was raging above German cities, industrial centres, transport hubs, and staging posts for German counterattacks. Yet war on both the western and eastern fronts had been going disastrously. The Nazi war machine did not have the resources to prosecute powerful enough offensives on both fronts at the same time. The Germans would have to alternate their campaigns on those theatres. The advance on one would be checked allowing for greater resources to be sent to the other. Hitler chose to try and supress the Allies in the west to allow for a later and concerted effort against the Red Army in the east.

Hitler needed time; not only to develop his wonder weapons, but also to rebalance the German war economy. His armaments ministry had been moving industry away from vulnerable locations in the Ruhr and Silesia to massive subterranean factories and plants squirreled away in Germany's inaccessible dark forests. And to recruit, retrain and reequip his troops after the German Army's mauling in France and on the Eastern Front after Operation Bagration, Russia' revenge for Operation Barbarossa. Hitler's strike in the Ardennes was Hitler's last major gamble. And one in which if successful and all goals were met the course of the war in the western theatre could have changed.

The building up of a massive strike force with the latest equipment, such as the Tiger II tank, was not the only weapon that Hitler used. He also hoped to employ another factor, that of fear. Hitler had ordered that the *Waffen*-SS must do whatever it takes to win.[2] It was thought that massacring American prisoners would not only allow the Germans to keep up a rapid advance because they would not have to deal with ferrying soldiers into captivity, but such acts would also demoralise American GIs. The reality when these plans were put into effect proved to be somewhat different.

The Battle

THE FIGHTING BEGAN on 16th December 1944 with a powerful artillery barrage aimed at the American front line. The Allies were also hit with Hitler's cunning plan to disrupt US forces behind their own lines. This did succeed in creating initial confusion, but the German operatives were soon identified and executed.

Within just two days, and two cold nights, the main German forces had penetrated as far as the town of Stavelot, twenty miles into what was once American held ground. In the process the American 106th and 28th Divisions had been swamped.

During the opening days of the battle Montgomery closely monitored the situation. Modelling his battlefield communications upon a system established by the Duke of Wellington, who used a team of riders to keep him in touch with events in the build-up to the Battle of Waterloo, Montgomery established a team of liaison officers that kept him informed of developments as the Germans attacked the Americans. Monty quickly saw that Bradley's 12th Army group had been cut in two by the onslaught. Recognising the seriousness of the situation he immediately made sure that the rear and southern flanks of the 21st Army Group, which was to the north of the German advance, was secure in case of a complete German breakthrough. Montgomery's armies had been preparing to engage the Germans in a battle to secure the Rhineland. He stopped this and began moving British forces into a position that would halt any German advance beyond the Meuse. XXX Corps, the only reserve available that was near to the German's northern flank, assumed the command of the Guards Armoured Division, 51st (Highland) Division, 43rd (Wessex) Infantry Division and 53rd (Welsh) Infantry Division. Along with three more armoured brigades this force drew up in the area around Louvain-St Trond and Turnhout.

General Bradley was taking action on the southern shoulder of the Battle of the Bulge. On 17th December Omar Bradley, also known as the GIs general or simply 'Brad', on the advice of General Middleton, identified the town of Bastogne, a place with good road links, as a key location that must be held.

On the northern shoulder the situation was still unclear. Montgomery sent troops south to gain more information and to prepare defences on the bridges over the Meuse from Liege to Givet. He also engaged the elite troops of the Special Air Service (SAS) in these operations sending them with the forces that he scraped together – staff from a tank replacement station – to the Namur-Giyet area. Monty also established armoured car patrols to keep communications open between Liege and Namur. He also rushed 29 Armoured Brigade from Western Belgium, where it was about to begin training with the new British Comet tank, to the Namur zone. Montgomery ordered them to take back their Shermans and move as quickly as possible. The Comet was a superb cruiser tank but the demands of the fight meant that crews were required to go into battle in the machines they knew.

The fighting was desperate, and the number of American casualties started to mount. These losses came from the fighting but also from the execution of prisoners of war. On 17th December, close to the Belgium town of Malmedy, more than 80 Americans of Battery B of the 285th Field Artillery Observation Battalion were massacred by the men of *Kampfgruppe* Peiper who were commanded by the famous tank ace Colonel Joachim Peiper. These forces were in the 1st SS Panzer Division.

Peiper described how his men had a lust for blood,

"*My unit was composed of many young fanatical soldiers. They had seen thousands of mangled corpses and their hatred of the enemy was such, I swear it, I could not always keep it under control.*"

The reality, however, was that this was a very cold and calculated action which included searching the prisoners, lining them up, then bringing up vehicles and then most were massacred. Those that survived the initial shooting were killed one-by-one. Some momentarily escaped but were then hunted down and murdered. The crux of the issue was that the Germans could not advance swiftly with prisoners of war as they would cause them delays. Joachim Peiper had orders to let nothing, and no one get in his way.

From the very start of the Battle of the Bulge Montgomery had been urging Eisenhower to keep the American focus on the fighting in the

Ardennes by putting the US forces far to the south, near to the Swiss border, on to the defensive. Monty was also suggesting that General Patton's Third Army should cancel its planned attack and immediately move north to attack the German's southern flank. This would rebalance the American forces along the lines Monty had been suggesting since the autumn.

On 18th December, with the German thrusts succeeding in advancing 20 miles into US lines, Eisenhower belatedly took the advice that had been suggested to him by Montgomery two months earlier. He ordered a halt to the offensive in the south and sought to plug the gap through which the Germans were pouring by ordering the Third Army to counter-attack the southern flank of the now rapidly expanding bulge. However, the Allies were being forced to fight the Germans when the Nazis had the initiative, under Montgomery's plan the Americans would have taken the offensive first and catch Hitler off-guard. That would have prevented the Führer's forces from achieving to achieve the element of surprise which was what the US complacent strategy allowed to occur. To make sure that US soldiers were better balanced, the Seventh Army was also moved further north to make the American 12th Army Group a more cohesive force. This was also suggested by Montgomery long before the Battle of the Bulge took place.

On 19th December the situation was continuing to deteriorate. There was a danger that advanced German mobile units could get through to the river Meuse, leaving the road to Brussels open. In 1940 the German crossing of that waterway was a key component in the Nazi victory over France. In not unfamiliar circumstances, four years later forces now facing the German Fifth Panzer Army were weak and overstretched. Just three days into the battle the Nazis had reached as far as La Roche-en-Ardenne, Marche and Hotton; creating a salient from Bastogne to Durbuy. In the event of a further American collapse Montgomery established units to secure the roads around the Belgian capital. Montgomery had now secured the area and was in a position to repel any German attack that crossed the Meuse. The ultimate objective of Hitler's attack was now unlikely to be reached by Hitler's panzers, yet the fighting had only just begun and many lives on all sides were still to be lost.

Despite making his own preparations Monty was still just an interested observer in the main battle to the south of his command. This, however, was about to change. On 20th December just 30 minutes before Monty was to begin an 11am conference with his two subordinate commanders in the 21st Army Group, Generals Crerar and Dempsey, he received a telephone call from General Eisenhower giving him overall command of all American forces north of the Bulge. This was General Simpson's US Ninth Army and General Hodges' First Army. They were under the overall direction of Bradley, but he had effectively lost control of these two armies as they had been cut-off from his headquarters in Luxembourg.

The decision on 20th to place these two armies under Monty's command was originally suggested by General Walter Bedell Smith, Eisenhower's Chief of Staff. According to the American army officer and military historian, Hugh Marshall Cole, this change of command, *'must have been difficult to make, since both Eisenhower and Smith were acutely conscious of the smoldering animosity toward the British in general and Montgomery in particular which existed in the 12th Army Group and Third Army, not to mention the chronic anti-British sentiment which might be anticipated from some circles in Washington.'*[3]

That same day Monty gave instructions to Simpson to meet him at First Army's HQ which Montgomery set out for at 12 noon. First Army were being subjected to vicious hammer blows from the German advance. Despite the desperate situation, the two isolated American armies had been neglected by General Bradley, who had failed to visit his two subordinates, nor even seek to coordinate the resistance of the two armies that were engaged with the Germans on the northern shoulder of the advance. Despite those glaring omissions, Bradley was incensed.

Montgomery entered the headquarters displaying his characteristic self-confidence. This attitude had been important to turning around the fortunes of the British Eighth Army in North Africa in 1942 where he came in brimming with confidence and rebuilt the morale of this beleaguered force that had suffered many defeats at the hands of Rommel but from then on the Eight Army knew only victory. Yet the American Generals found this self-assured style to be evocative of a conquering hero come to laud over the embattled American commanders. Yet the reality was that he took charge in his own inimitable style and developed a strategy that delivered victory.

Eisenhower kept Monty informed as to the unfolding situation in the other areas and sought his advice. When Ike spoke to Montgomery via radio, he was thinking of his earlier conference with his American Commanders where he said that the Battle of the Bulge was a good opportunity for the Allies. He had said that "*the present situation is to be regarded as one of opportunity for us and not of disaster.*" He then said to Montgomery, the man he was about to use to turn the crisis to a victory that, "*Our weakest spot is in the direction of Namur. The general plan is to plug the holes in the north and launch co-ordinated attack from the south.* Later on, Eisenhower contacted Montgomery again, asking him to "*Please let me have your personal appreciation of the situation on the north flank with reference to the possibility of giving up, if necessary, some ground in order to shorten our line and collect a strong reserve for the purpose of destroying the enemy in Belgium.*"[4] Eisenhower recognised that the main danger to the Americans was on the northern shoulder. What is more, intelligence reports suggested that there may be more attacks further to the north to attempt what is known as a double envelopment of the allied forces in that sector.

Seeing the northern shoulder of the German advance as a complete front, rather than individual units trying to hold their ground, Monty reorganised the Allied war machine. Montgomery and his Supreme Commander both agreed as to how the conflict should be handled. With the complete support of General Eisenhower, Montgomery did not simply throw divisions into the battle as soon as they could be rushed to the scene. This would have meant that they would have been crushed by the German advance and even if such individual offensives had succeeded in halting the German steamroller there would not be adequate resources for a sustained counterattack. A more organised response was needed. Montgomery, in characteristic fashion visited his subordinates, appraised the situation, developed a strategy, and then put his plan into action.

Monty initially identified strong defensive points where the thrust could be stopped and reinforced strategic areas. Simultaneously, Montgomery began the process of building up American reserves that could take part in a counterattack when he deemed that they would have a decisive effect. To this end he decided that the VII Corps of the US First Army should become the reserve force that can take the offensive. They mustered to the north-west of the Belgian town of Marche. This was to prove a useful place for this rested and regrouped corps as they were soon to play an important part in the fighting.

British soldiers first took part in this conflict when Montgomery joined them to the Ninth Army to bolster its defence and allow the Ninth to take over part of the territory defended by First Army. This action stabilised the front line which was increasingly becoming secure as British troops were also used as reserves to the rear of the US First and Ninth Armies.

On 20th December, whilst Montgomery was reorganising the front facing the main German attacks, Eisenhower continued shifting the focus of US forces towards the Ardennes region. He ordered General Devers' 6th Army Group to move north to fill the area up to Saarlautern and to take up the defensive. This enabled Bradley's 12th Army Group to concentrate more of its fire power in the vicinity of Bastogne and Luxembourg and counterattack the underbelly of the German bulge.

The Sixth Panzer Army concentrated its ferocious attacks using I Corps against the Americans in the area around Malmedy and Stavelot. The Germans hoped to be able to reach Liège by passing through the devastated American lines and drive their II Corps of the SS through the hole. Yet they were breaking themselves on what was now a better organised sector. Montgomery had checked the advance in this front at much cost to the Germans. And on 22nd December the II Corps of the SS sought a new way forward. von Rundstedt's forces now hoped to capture Liège by moving II Corps further to the west from where it could attack the city from Durbuy which was to the south of their objective.

The moving of II Corps of the SS further west led them to the area between Marche and Hotton, where they ran into VII Corps which Montgomery had posted to this area. The fighting between the two was soon underway. The repositioning of British forces to secure the ground even further to the west was also important. The area from Dinant north to Namur was covered by the British 29th Armoured Brigade which Montgomery had rushed back from their refitting, and they fought against the German spearhead which was by 23rd December just 12 miles east of Dinant.

During this time the battle for Saint Vith was erupting. The town of Sankt Vith, as it is known to its denizens, and its road links made the area an important transport centre. Incidentally, the residents of this Belgian area spoke German as their first language. Saint Vith was at the centre of an Allied salient within the German bulge. It was more than a thorn in the side of the Sixth Panzer Army; in fact, it was holding up their entire advance and prevented effective coordination between the two panzer armies in the north. It was now receiving Field Marshal Model's full attention and he wanted it eliminated. The defence of Saint Vith was one of the epic struggles in the Battle of the Bulge where US soldiers were holding out against the odds; however, time was running out for them, and the troops hold on Saint Vith was coming to an end with the city on the verge of collapse indeed resistance was being annihilated. Montgomery had already ordered 7th Armoured Division to withdraw. Monty's order to the commander in the town, General Robert Hasbrouck, read, '*You have accomplished your mission – a mission well-done – it is time to withdraw.*'[5]

The decision to leave Saint Vith not only saved the GIs in the emerging pocket from destruction but it also fitted in with Montgomery's strategy of tidying up American lines to make them impregnable and enable US troops to avoid a wider encirclement. Ultimately, the stubborn defence of the town had served its military purpose as it had held the Germans back for longer than could be reasonably expected and gave the Allied forces behind it time to prepare. And those positions could now be further reinforced by the troops who had been in Saint Vith. It is worth noting that the German plan to capture this strategically important town called for it to be taken on day two of operations; 17th December 1944. Many days had been lost fighting in and around the municipality.

The fighting continued around the Belgian town of Ciney and the village of Celles, Houyet which was reached by the Germans on Christmas Day 1944. Hitler's forces were just four miles from the river Meuse, yet the 26th December was the high tide of their advance as their major assault in the north was stopped in its tracks. The US 2nd Armoured Division fighting alongside the British 29th Armoured Brigade had halted the Nazi advance. The Germans suffered many casualties. Yet the Axis assault had still inflicted numerous Allied losses and caused major disruption in their lines splitting the Americans and creating a salient that stretched for more than 250 miles bulging into territory that was once held by 12th Army Group. The bulge still had to be eliminated.

There were limited opportunities for Allied air power to conduct sorties against the German ground forces from early on in the campaign and there were some dogfights but these were few in number. However, Christmas Eve 1944 saw the skies clear and the deadly firepower of American and British tactical bombers now rained down on the panzers. The lack of cloud cover at night, however, led to excessively cold weather which made the days freezing as well. That said, by Christmas Day the military situation was looking much better for the Allies. All the possible paths to the Meuse were sealed-off. Eisenhower had wanted the Germans to be stopped at that river; Montgomery had made sure that they did not even reach the symbolic and strategic channel. The Germans, however, still held on in a front which stretched from Bastogne linking to St Hubert and on to Hotton, Marche-en-Famenne, Malmedy to the Elsenborn Ridge. Holding the forces of the Sixth Panzer Army at this ridge prevented the Germans from capturing the supply depots and the fuel which they held to fuel hungry vehicles. It also halted the Germans from taking advantage of the road network that lay beyond the ridge.

General Bradley visited Montgomery at his Headquarters on Christmas Day to consult with the British Field Marshal. At this meeting Bradley received a dressing down from Montgomery for his part in allowing this sorry situation to develop. Montgomery said,

"*it was entirely our fault we had gone too far with our right; we had tried to develop two thrusts at the same time, and neither had been strong enough to gain decisive results. The enemy saw his chance and took it. Now we were in a proper muddle*".[6]

The situation was still desperate, yet Montgomery had not lost his own individual sense of humour. In a report to the Prime Minister and Field Marshal Alan Brooke, the Chief of the Imperial General Staff (CIGS), he explained the situation and what he was doing about it. At the end he wrote, '*We cannot come out through Dunkirk this time as the Germans still hold that place*'. This was not considered funny. When the telegram was presented to Churchill by the CIGS the final sentence was removed. This was not to be the last time that Monty's ill-thought through messages were to raise the eyebrows of his superiors. Following the Battle of the Bulge Montgomery had to apologise to Eisenhower for causing offensive by overly pushing for his strategic vision to be adopted.

Confidence amongst the British Army was high. Montgomery, throughout his career visited his subordinates to make sure that they knew their role, this characteristic and desire to communicate continued in the Battle of the Bulge. Monty went to see Lieutenant-General Brian Horrocks commander of XXX Corps, part of the British Second Army, to make sure his units would hold the Meuse between Namur and Louvain. Horrocks had different ideas. Noticing that the site of the 1815 Battle of Waterloo was close by, Horrocks suggested that the Germans should be allowed to cross the strategically important river Meuse and reach the Belgium town of Waterloo. Then he could deliver a victory over the Germans on the same field where Wellington defeated Napoleon. Germany's forcing a crossing of that river further upstream four years before proved to be a vital manoeuvre and was fundamental to German success against France in 1940. Montgomery disagreed with his long-serving and loyal subordinate, Monty ordered Lieutenant-General Miles Dempsey, the commander of Second Army, to make sure that Horrocks did not allow any Germans to get beyond the river Meuse.

XXX Corps did the job that Montgomery asked of them and had a key role in holding the bridges. This powerful formation also drove the German panzer's out of the Belgium town of Celles on 27th December.

The next day, on 28th December, Eisenhower visited Montgomery in the Belgian city of Hasselt. At this meeting Monty kept Eisenhower informed about the attacks which he was making against the northern flank of the bulge. He also gave the Supreme Commander the details on the build-up of the forces that were to be used in the general offensive which Monty was going to direct towards the town of Houffalize in the centre of the salient which the Germans had recently created in the Ardennes Offensive. Whilst the forces for this counter blow were being prepared Eisenhower and Montgomery agreed that the strategy was to prepare for a renewed German attack, Allied intelligence predicted that this would come in the north. The defences in this shoulder were secure and the vital areas that lay beyond the bulge were safely out of reach to the Germans but work still needed to be done to resist the expected renewed

German assault that would use replacement soldiers that were rested and had not been worn down by the near fortnight of continued operations. The two Allied commanders then agreed that if no more major German attacks came in the north then preparations for the major counterattack can continue. They agreed that this should begin early on 3rd January.

By New Year's Eve 1944 General Horrock's XXX Corps had captured Rochefort, blunting the German advance and also beginning in earnest the process of driving the Nazis back, within the space of a few days. Previously historians have thought that Montgomery only began offensive action in January yet the attacks of XXX Corps show that this long held belief is not correct. These attacks were however limited by the fact that the need to commit the US VII Corps to the battle and the sheer ferocity of the fighting on the northern shoulder of the German advance meant that there were few reserves to use in the counterstrike. To create the forces that Montgomery needed to drive the Germans back, and out, of the bulge. Monty moved XXX Corps to the area between Givet in France, and Hotton in Belgium. This transfer was concluded on 2nd January 1945 and enabled VII Corps to move towards the strategic town of Houffalize. This began the very next day. In this action they intended to link up with the Third Army's advance coming from the south.

During this time, when the British armoured forces were being repositioned, the air battle was to take a new twist. Allied air attacks had been continuing unabated and were taking a heavy toll on the Germans; death from above was their nemesis. Hitler recognised this and ordered what he hoped would be a decisive attack by the Luftwaffe that would eliminate the Allied air superiority over the Battle of the Bulge. This attack from the Jagdwaffe, the Luftwaffe's fighter force, came on New Year's Day, 1st January 1945, and was codenamed Operation *Bodenplatte*. This was originally intended to support the German attacks earlier in the battle, now it was needed to save the *Waffen*-SS and the *Heer*, the German Army, from destruction and give the Luftwaffe the advantage. The air attacks came against Royal Air Force, the Royal Canadian Air Force (RCAF) and US Airforce bases in the Netherlands, Belgium, and France. The main targets were airbases closest to the bulge in particular those to its north where Montgomery was in command.

It was on 1st January 1945 that Montgomery's personal plane, which had been lent to him by General Eisenhower, was '*shot to pieces*'. Eisenhower was kind enough to immediately replace it with a transport that was originally meant to be for Eisenhower himself. Montgomery wrote to thank Eisenhower on 6th January, the letter read,

'*Such spontaneous kindness touches me deeply and from my heart I send you my grateful thanks. If there is anything I can ever do for you to ease the tremendous burden that you bear you know you have only to command me. And I want you to know that I shall always stand firmly behind you in everything you do.*'

Operation *Bodenplatte* did achieve tactical surprise and inflicted losses on the USAAF, the RAF, and the RCAF. However, it led to a far greater loss of German fighters and the destruction of what was left of German airpower at a time when both men and machines could not be replaced. Many of these aeroplanes were not only destroyed by their Allied counterparts. The German flak corps, which was there to defend the ground troops from air strikes, opened up on their own planes, shooting many of them out of the sky. They had not been told to expect the Luftwaffe's Jagdwaffe aircraft to be flying above them. Maintaining operational secrecy can at times lead to catastrophic mistakes being made. Ultimately Operation *Bodenplatte* amounted to another futile sacrifice which only hastened the inevitable defeat of the Third Reich.

On 3rd January, right on schedule, VII Corps began its attacks. The Germans, despite being forced to abandon their mobile warfare, were not about to admit defeat and retreat. Through using anti-tank weapons and even tanks which they dug-in to form strong points, they had learned how to go over to the defensive and deny the Allies their advance. What's more , on 3rd January the appalling weather, which marred the winter of 1944/45, returned. This restricted visibility to no more than several hundred yards. Despite those conditions an advance of approaching several miles was made. However, the offensive had to be halted for two days after a severe snowstorm.

XXX Corps launched another attack with two divisions on 4th January and continued to bludgeon back the furthest advance into the bulge. The British 6th Airborne Division, which had been rushed to the scene to take up the defensive, joined the attack. The Belgium village of Bure was taken by 5th January.

The offensive by VII Corps began again after two days on 5th January and despite there still being bad weather VII Corps, supported by the US XVIII Airborne Corps, had achieved much success. They seized territory south-east of Grandmenil cutting the road between Vielsalm and La Roche-en-Ardenne which the Germans were relying upon to supply their forces in the north. The 82nd Airborne Division reached the villages of Vielsalm and Salmchâteau on 7th January. Whilst VII Corps were attacking there was a simultaneous offensive from the British 53rd Division which took Grimbiermont and the strategically important heights to the east of the town on 7th January.

The situation for the Germans in the north had deteriorated massively. They were well on their way to being defeated by Montgomery. Yet Hitler was not about to give up. Military logic clearly dictated that if it was not possible to bounce a crossing of the river Meuse in the initial stages of the attack, then the Allies would make this impossible after the element of surprise had been lost. Despite this seemingly obvious scenario being true, Hitler kept up the pressure for three weeks and brought into the fray what remained of his reserves, troops that were needed to defend the Fatherland were wasted in a renewed assault. Now that the attack on the northern shoulder of the bulge had failed the Germans sought to launch new attacks to the south-west. Nor had they ceased their futile efforts to capture Bastogne which was attracting more German divisions like moths to a flame.

Montgomery was directing his forces in the north towards Houffalize, and the resistance from the Germans was stiff. To keep up the momentum Monty put 51st Armoured Division into the fight, taking point from 53rd Division. They had the immediate objective of advancing towards La-Roche-en-Ardenne and Champlon in southern Belgium. Monty set the river Ourthe, which runs from near Houffalize to Liège where it joins up with the Meuse, as the limit of XXX Corp's advance. La-Roche-en-Ardenne was liberated on 10th January. The 6th Airborne Division reached Saint-Hubert on 11th January and linked up with the western side of Third Army.

On 13th January the situation was so desperate for the Germans that the town of Saint Vith was being approached by XVIII Airborne Corps who were attacking from the west. The town, devastated by not only the initial German attacks but also by the US counterattack as well as Allied bombing, was finally retaken by the allies on 23rd January 1945. The 51st Armoured Division was also breaking out from La-Roche-en-Ardenne and advancing south.

As the Battle of the Bulge entered its final phase with victory just a few days away Montgomery went to lengths to try and get on with his American opposite number, Omar Bradley and his subordinate General Patton. On 14th January, Monty wrote to General Bradley. His message read,

'*My dear Brad,*
It does seem as if the battle of the 'salient' will shortly be drawing to a close, and when it is all clean and tidy I imagine that your armies will be returning to your operational command.

I would like to say two things:
First: What a great honour it has been for me to command such fine troops.
Second: How well they have all done.
It has been a great pleasure to work with Hodges and Simpson; both have done very well.

And the Corps Commanders in the First Army (Gerow, Collins, Ridgeway) have been quite magnificent; it must be most exceptional to find such a good lot of Corps Commanders gathered together in one Army.

All of us in the northern side of the salient would like to say how much we have admired the operations that have been conducted on the southern side; if you had not held on firmly to Bastogne the whole situation might have become very awkward.
My kind regards to you and to George Patton.
Yrs very sincerely,
B L Montgomery'

On 16th January, Third and First armies linked up at Houffalize and the Allies then drove east eliminating the German salient as they went, retaking much of the land that had been lost at the expense of many fallen US soldiers, in the opening days of the conflict. Monty's and Bradley's American forces now ultimately aimed to push the Germans further back behind the lines from where they had started the Battle of the Bulge. The battle was now effectively won, Montgomery then wrote to General Eisenhower. His letter read,

'I have great pleasure in reporting to you that the task you gave me in the Ardennes is now concluded. First and Third Armies have joined hands at Houffalize and are advancing eastwards. It can therefore be said that we have now achieved tactical victory within the salient. I am returning First Army to Bradley tomorrow as ordered by you. I would like to say what a great pleasure it has been to have such a splendid army under my command and how very well it has done.'

On 17th January Eisenhower replied to Montgomery, writing as follows,

'Thank you again for the way you pitched in to help out during the German thrust. Some day I hope I can show my appreciation in a more lasting manner.'

By 18th January, as well as the forces advancing east from Houffalize, in the north the First Army was driving eastwards from Stavelot and Malmedy towards the area between Monschau and Saint Vith. And in the South the Third Army was approaching Vianden from the south-west.

Following the Battle of the Bulge, Montgomery moved the British troops that were taking part out of operations to support the Americans in the Ardennes and repositioned those crown forces to prepare for the subjugation of the Rhineland.

To support operations in the Battle of the Bulge the Germans tried to unbalance the Allies by launching attacks against the American forces to the south of the salient in the Alsace and Lorraine region of France. This was known as Operation *Nordwind*. It was hoped that this would force Eisenhower to shift troops from the main fighting in Belgium to the south. This greatly alarmed General de Gaulle who was worried that the French city of Strasbourg may come under attack. On 3rd January he threatened to withdraw the French army from Eisenhower's overall command and act independently to defend Strasbourg, yet this would mean taking them out from positions where they can support future offensive operations. Eisenhower threatened to cut-off all supplies to the French if de Gaulle did this and pointed out that the French had allowed this situation to develop by their failure to eliminate the Germans in the south who held on around the city of Colmar which is to the south of Strasbourg. Yet Eisenhower sought to accommodate him by moving some troops from the north to make Strasbourg safe. This pleased de Gaulle.

This was not the only time when Eisenhower's undoubted diplomatic skills would be tested during the Battle of the Bulge.

The Allies at war: The Infamous Press Conference

HITLER'S PLAN IN the Battle of the Bugle had been to divide and conquer Britain and America. Physically separating the British commanded forces from those from the United States would, he hoped, lead to a political division. This was fantasy and desperate wishful thinking yet misreported and misunderstood comments from Montgomery nearly resulted in causing a schism between Montgomery and the Americans.

On 7th January 1945 Montgomery held a press conference to talk about the battle and stop the reports in the British press that were criticising Eisenhower's handling of the war which had arguably allowed this crisis to develop. Monty had approval to hold the press conference from the British Prime Minister, Winston Churchill.

The final and most salient points in his talk to the assembled press were intended to plead for the journalists not to damage *"Allied solidarity"*. He explained to them that,

"*It is team-work that pulls you through dangerous times; it is team-work that wins battles; it is victories in battle that win wars… Nothing must be done by anyone that tends to break down the team spirit of our Allied team; if you try and 'get at' the captain of the team you are liable to induce a loss of confidence, and this may spread and have disastrous results. I would say that anyone who tries to break up the team spirit of the Allies is definitely helping the enemy. Let me tell you that the captain of our team is Eisenhower. I am absolutely devoted to Ike; we are the greatest of friends. It grieves me when I see uncomplimentary articles about him in the British press; he bears a great burden, he needs our fullest support, he has a right to expect it, and it is up to all of us to see that he gets it.*"

How could such an innocently intended press conference result in such controversy? The team spirit did not stretch as far as some American generals such as the overtly Anglophobe General Patton and his commander General Bradley, almost equally suspicious of the British and still smarting from losing two whole armies to his rival from the United Kingdom.

Montgomery did praise the GIs stating quite clearly that *"Rundstedt was really beaten by the good fighting qualities of the American soldier and by the team-work of the Allies."* He went further in paying tribute to the Americans, explaining his high opinion of the American soldier. Stating, *"He is a brave fighting man, steady under fire, and with that tenacity in battle which stamps the first class soldier… I salute the brave fighting men of America; I never want to fight alongside better soldiers…"*

Yet that was not enough to appease Montgomery's opposite numbers in command of other American armies in the field whom, apart from Eisenhower, he had failed to mention. This omission from his briefing was an oversight that was to rankle US commanders which he had forsaken to acknowledge let alone praise the part they played in dealing with this German attack.

Montgomery also said that *"The battle has been most interesting; I think possibly one of the most interesting and tricky battles I have ever handled, with great issues at stake."* Describing the battle as *"interesting"* was seen as being disrespectful to the 80,000 casualties that the American's had suffered in what was for them a desperate and bloody battle. Yet Montgomery was not only a soldier and commander he was also a military theorist who had a scholarly interest in his chosen profession – warfare. Whilst the American generals were dejected after the mauling they had suffered; Montgomery, a man who was not slow to express his self-belief and tell others about his successes, appeared to them to be victorious over the Americans when in reality Monty was jubilant that he had beaten the Germans.

Whereas Eisenhower and his American subordinates had left themselves open to a military attack, Montgomery's press conference had also left him open to a cunning German attack. Joseph Goebbels, the Nazi Minister of Propaganda, seized on a report to the BBC about the press conference from the Australian war correspondent, Chester Wilmot. The transmission was then re-worked to make Monty's words appear to be anti-American and then aired by the German propaganda machine. Staff in General Bradley's Headquarters heard the fake news report and fell for the trick. Believing that the distorted words were a BBC broadcast the anger was unleashed which then took on its own momentum.[7]

That being the case Montgomery still regretted holding the press conference, saying;

"*So great was the feeling against me on the part of the American generals, that whatever I said was bound to be wrong. I should therefore have said nothing.*"[8]

Whereas many American Generals thought that Monty had intentionally demeaned them, Eisenhower '*did not believe that Montgomery meant his words as they sounded.*' Yet the strength of feeling was so great that the other American generals began a campaign of voicing '*reciprocal scorn and contempt.*'[9] It seems that this lasted for many years.

However, did this infamous press conference, or to be more precise the reaction that Montgomery's words caused, undermine Montgomery's influence on how the future course of the war will be handled?

Aftermath

THE STORM THAT was created following the Montgomery press conference insinuates that despite his military success Monty had lost the political battle with his US comrades; but is that actually the case? The evidence suggests otherwise. It has long been believed that once the crisis of the Battle of the Bulge was over the two American armies that were assigned to Monty were returned to Bradley's command. Yet that was not what happened. The US Ninth Army was actually transferred from Bradley's 12th Army Group to Montgomery's 21st Army Group and would be used in conjunction with his other British and Canadian armies in operations aimed at reaching the Rhine and driving into the Ruhr. Montgomery's 21st Army Group and his intended northern thrust into Germany's industrial heartland and onto the North German Plain was, far from being stymied for political reasons, actually emboldened. When it came to the major operation to cross the Rhine in March 1945 Eisenhower made Montgomery's 21st Army Group the main thrust into the heart of Nazi Germany.

Furthermore, Montgomery did win plaudits for his handling of the Battle of the Bulge. Bradley recognised his "*notable contribution*". Fulsome praise also came from the American Major General Matt Ridgway. He was the commander of the US XVIII Airborne Corps. He wrote to Montgomery and his letter read,

'*It has been an honoured privilege and a very great personal pleasure to have served, even so briefly, under your distinguished leadership. To the gifted professional guidance you at once gave me, was added your own consummate courtesy and consideration. I am deeply grateful for both. My warm and sincere good wishes will follow you and with them the hope of again serving you in pursuit of a common goal.*'[10]

The Battle of the Bulge severely damaged Hitler's war machine. Just like in 1918 when in World War I the German forces attacked the British in what was called the Kaiser's Battle, the only lasting effect was to use up their own resources that could not by then be replaced. The Battle of the Bulge led to Hitler losing 600 assault guns and tanks, 1,600 planes,

6,000 transport vehicles, and Germany had suffered perhaps as many as 120,000 lost. However, the Nazi commanders only acknowledged 90,000 casualties, which is still a massive butcher's bill. Yet the Americans also suffered a bloody nose. Eisenhower estimated that 733 tank and tank destroyers were out of action with 77,000 casualties which consisted of 21,000 missing or captured, 48,000 wounded and 8,000 killed in action.11

The loss of men and materiel was not the only way in which the Allies had been set back by Hitler's attack on the Ardennes. Time had also been lost. The need to eliminate the German bulge held back Allied offensives against more strategic targets by as much as six weeks. Time that could have been used to develop the advance towards the Rhine. Furthermore, if basic precautions had been taken the Battle of the Bulge and the resulting mass American casualties need not have taken place. The Americans also lost impetus in the coal rich Saar which was arguably far more strategically significant to the Allies.

The need to be prepared for further German attacks in support of the operations aimed at Antwerp and the British role in fighting back against the German attacks delayed the introduction of the British Comet tank. The Christmas period of 1944 had been earmarked as a time when tank crews in the 21st Army Group would begin training in this new British cruiser tank. When it eventually came into use during the British advance across Germany this agile, powerful, and well protected tank finally allowed Britain's armoured divisions to more than match the German panzers. Being able to introduce the Comet earlier would have been a boon for the British advance.

In the latter stages of the Second World War, when the Allies had learnt to deal with the blitzkrieg, German attacks, most notably at the Kursk salient and then the Battle of Bulge, had ultimately only succeeded in using up valuable resources which sped up the defeat of the One Thousand Year Reich.

Hitler's plan was bold, and it understood, perhaps better than the Allied Supreme Commander himself, the fundamental importance of the port of Antwerp. It sought to strike at a proven weak spot and eliminate the main source of supply which was enabling the Allies deliver their material advantage. Yet ultimately it proved to be a reckless gamble that was begun without the resources to make it successful. The strategic objective of Brussels and then Antwerp was therefore thoroughly unrealistic. German war aims just wrought more pain.

The Germans that carried out the massacre near Malmedy were tortured after being captured towards the end of the war and later sentenced to death by a military tribunal. Yet later, as there were fears that their convictions were unsafe, they had their sentences commuted to prison. Peiper would be sentenced to hang for his crimes, but legal technicalities led him to serve only a brief period in gaol. Extra-judicial 'justice' was later meted out by French anti-fascists who murdered him at his home in France in July 1976 when firebombs were thrown into his house; leaving behind the charred corpse of an old man. Sepp Dietrich, the commander of Sixth Panzer Army, also received a prison sentence. During the Battle of the Bulge the Americans also took retaliation against captured *Waffen*-SS soldiers, taking the lives of some prisoners in a manner outside the laws of war.

Ultimately an attack on the scale of the Battle of the Bulge was not warranted. A case can be made for a smaller attack to unbalance the western Allies and forestall the Anglo-American winter offensives. Yet to place at risk the enormous resources which the German High Command had so painstakingly put together was beyond reason. It risked too much on an attack which had at best a limited chance of success. What is more, when success was clearly beyond the Germans, after the route to the Meuse was denied to them, the offensive should have been called-off. However, Hitler ordered renewed attacks compounding his strategic mistake. Using up both men and materiel that at this stage in the war could not be replaced. Montgomery wrote that after the Battle of Bulge '*the Germans gave no serious resistance.*'[12] The German failure in the Ardennes Offiensive and the valuable resources which this major operation used up meant that the Nazi regime now lacked the strength to defend the Fatherland. And the war was then brought to an end six months earlier than it would otherwise have finished. It also showed the limitations of German power in relation to that now possessed by its enemies, a massive contrast to when still fresh in the memories of the combatants the Germans had bounced a victory over France.

Did the failure of the Battle of the Bulge lead to Hitler abandoning his reckless gambling? Hitler did not change and in March 1945 he ordered a similar attack against the Soviets even using forces that had failed earlier in the west. The Battle of the Bulge was not the last time that the Sixth Panzer Army was to sacrifice itself in a futile attack. After the failed Ardennes offensive, Hitler moved this now much depleted force to Hungary where it was ordered to take part in an offensive against the Red Army. This panzer 'army' could have been used in the defence of Berlin, however, in the Lake Balaton Offensive Hitler's recognition of the economic aspects of war led him to divert the Sixth Panzer Army to defend oil production in the west of Hungary launching it into yet another self-defeating offensive.

Despite the aim of this great clash being to free up resources, like the objective of the Battle of the Bulge, to fight back against the Red Army in the east, it actually weakened that front as well. The movement of men from the Eastern Front and the sacrificing of its weapons of war in the Battle of the Bulge actually made the Russian advance on Berlin less difficult than it would otherwise have been. The real winner was therefore Joseph Stalin.

Why the Allies Won

MONTGOMERY WAS OF the opinion that although the Germans initially drove the Americans back, giving them what he called a '*bloody nose*', the Allies under his control quickly regained their composure. The Germans were then met with forces that were well balanced and prepared to meet the challenge. And when the Germans had lost the initiative, the Allies drove them out of the bulge which the German offensive had created.

Despite the salient in the American lines being formed within just a matter of days the German advance was still too slow. They needed to establish bridgeheads over the river Meuse within the initial few days of the battle before cohesive opposition was established. The Germans did of course eventually try to reach the river and take the crossing points but they failed to concentrate their spearheads into powerful enough formations that would be able to deliver success. These were then surrounded and eliminated or thrown back from where they had to regroup before another attack could be launched, costing the Germans yet more time. The Fifth Panzer Army did not use the little time it had well; it waited for its counterpart, the Sixth Panzer Army, instead of moving forward as quickly as possible and then found that the road network was incapable of supporting the swift movement of two major forces. Whilst the attack across the Ardennes gave success to the Führer in 1940, it was not to restore Nazi power when this route was used again just over four and a half years later. The situation in 1944 was a very different one from four years before . In 1940 despite the Germans encountering severe traffic jams when attacking across the Ardennes, Allied incompetence meant that this did not disadvantage the Axis attack. However, in 1944 the Germans could not count on such weak leadership.

Furthermore, the *Waffen*-SS and the *Heer* did not enjoy the same quality of air support that it once had. In 1940 the German attack was towards the South-west which followed the road network. However, in 1944 the offensive was aimed at Antwerp, towards the North-West, which ran across the road infrastructure. The attack did not enjoy the advantages of efficient links running in the direction of the advance.

There was also a major difference between the belligerents in late 1944. The Anglo-American armies had a massive advantage in the sheer mass of resources which they could put into the field of combat. The Germans may have had an advantage in the quality of their armoured vehicles, in particular the tanks, and in the skill of their fighting men. Montgomery thought that their soldiers were superior to that of their Allied counterparts and if the Germans were to be engaged on equal terms, then the Nazis would be victorious. However, despite their arguable individual merit, quantity has a quality all its own.

Despite most Allied soldiers taking part in the Battle of Bulge being American, British forces did play an important part in the victory. They allowed for hard-pressed US troops to be withdrawn from the fray and reform as a strategic reserve that could strike back against the Germans and make the Nazis pay for their reckless attack.

Ultimately Montgomery concluded that victory was not possible without the stubborn defence of the American soldiers especially at various towns in the path of the German thrusts notably Saint Vith and Bastogne.[13] These not only drew German strength away from the dash for Antwerp where it was most needed but also deprived the panzers of important road links compelling the enemy to take long diversions further slowing down the advance. Ultimately, the Sixth Panzer Army was effectively destroyed as a viable fighting unit as it was worn down against the forces under Montgomery's control. The Ardennes Offensive was not an effective lightning war and time ran out for Hitler.

The killing of American prisoners of war was also an important factor. Far from discouraging the US soldiers, the killing of American POWs actually encouraged the US troops to fight back even harder.

The powerful German tanks were effective at the start of the battle but in the long run they proved to be self-defeating. The Tiger and even heavier Tiger II tanks guzzled petrol, they did not use more efficient diesel engines. Fuel supplies were difficult to come by and many of the panzers ran out of petrol and had to be abandoned.

Another important factor was that although the Luftwaffe was still a threat, as had been shown during the New Year's Day Operation

Bodenplatte attack, they were incapable of protecting the German armour from allied air attacks; the Germans now lacked sufficient fighter cover and suffered from a paucity of pilots that were trained to use the planes properly. Without this air support, the 1944 offensive across the Ardennes was always going to fail. Montgomery was an early advocate of a combined arms approach to warfare teaching it as early as the 1930s. In the battles across France this doctrine came into its own. The Allies' ground attack aircraft mercilessly attacked the panzers from above with their Thunderbolts, Typhoons, and Mosquitos. The Battle of the Bulge was to be no different, as soon as the skies had cleared the threat from above materialised. The Germans on the ground had no answer to this and tactical bombers were, according to Montgomery, the German army's '*greatest terror*.

Appraising the myths of the Battle of the Bulge

MONTY HAS BEEN accused by some historians of unnecessarily delaying a counterattack against the Germans attacking from the northern shoulder. The reality of the situation was that the strategy had been agreed with Eisenhower. Anglo-American forces were to primarily remain on the defensive as the Wehrmacht, who were using most of their strength against Montgomery's command, broke itself on the reformed Allied lines. Furthermore, the date for the main counterattack, which was launched on 3rd January, was also agreed with General Eisenhower. In fact, as soon as Montgomery took over command, he started to organise US forces to launch this counterstrike.

Hollywood has presented its own take on this battle, in particular the role of General Patton. Whilst it is correct that he attacked the southern shoulder of the bulge from the south it is wrong to show this as the area where the main part of the battle was raging. Nor was the attack the main instrument of decision. As was originally planned the most powerful German spearheads were attacking north-west with the main blows in the first part of the conflict falling on the northern shoulder, away from Patton's area of operations. Hollywood's 'history' also has Patton prepared for the fight which he had pre-planned and executed in a swift and decisive thrust saving the forces in Bastogne.

The reality is that Patton had his heart set on the offensive towards the Saar which would now have to be postponed. He protested that he would now have to, under plans developed by his superior General Bradley, attack the German forces in the bulge. The date and direction of this attack was actually decided by Eisenhower, the Supreme Commander, and Patton's other commander, Omar Bradley. Patton's suggested plan was, as expressed to Eisenhower and Bradley at their conference on 19th December, to let the German advance continue. He said,

"*Hell, let's have the guts to let the bastards go all the way to Paris. Then we'll really cut'em off and chew 'em up.*"

This cavalier attitude was also supported by General Horrocks, the commander of XXX Corps. Paris, however, was not Hitler's aim. Instead, it was the strategically important port of Antwerp which was vital to relieving the Allies chronic supply problems and the Führer knew that this was of enormous importance to the future of his Reich. In fact, Patton not only misjudged the direction of the German attack, but he also underestimated its power. According to Eisenhower Patton '*did not seem to comprehend*' their strength. Once ordered north Patton promised a quick victory. However, Patton found that instead of delivering a rapid and decisive drive his attack was slow and laborious. And on several occasions Patton phoned Eisenhower '*to express his disappointment*' with the progress of his Third Army. In fact he had failed to fulfil his prediction that he would reach Bastogne in his initial push. This was especially disappointing because the German divisions in the south of the bulge were the weakest in the battle. Eisenhower, however, was comfortable with this because he knew that reaching Bastogne would be a hard slog and that Patton's initial estimates of how quickly the Third Army could advance were unrealistic.[14]

What is more, it is interesting to note that Bastogne had already been secured by the well supplied airborne troops who possessed artillery. Not one of the besieged 101st Airborne Division defending that municipality has stated that Patton saved them.

The Seventh Army, which was being attacked by Patton's Third Army, did suffer severe losses – just like the other German formations in the battle – but succeeded in escaping encirclement and was able to take part in the defence of the Reich.

Timeline:
The Battle of the Bulge at a Glance

16th December 1944
The German attack begins
The three armies launch their artillery and armoured assault on the weakened American positions. German covert operations also begin.

17th December
The Malmedy Massacre
The *Waffen*-SS kill American prisoners of war.
Bradley recognises the importance of Bastogne
General Omar Bradley authorises the defence of the town of Bastogne.
Montgomery begins taking precautions
The British Field Marshal employs the SAS to monitor the situation facing the American armies.

18th December
German forces reach Stavelot
The Panzers have advanced 20 miles. Prior to taking Stavelot the Germans had already captured; Mürringen, and Losheimergraben the day before.
101st Airborne Division arrive in Bastogne
On the orders of General Bradley American troops secure Bastogne a day before the Germans reach the area around the town.
Eisenhower reorganises the Allied armies
On the advice of Monty, Eisenhower cancels other offensives to concentrate on the battle in the Ardennes and changes the position of the US armies to make the front more secure.

19th December
Montgomery secures key defensive positions
Montgomery moved British forces to make sure that the Germans could not exploit any crossing of the Meuse River.

20th December
Eisenhower gives Montgomery command
Montgomery takes over control of the American First and Ninth Armies. He begins to reorganise the front, begins visiting the formations now under his control and designates VII Corps as a reserve that can take part in a counterattack.

21st December
Third Army moves north
Third Army begins the advance towards Bastogne.
Saint Vith evacuated
After holding up the German advance US troops, their job done, but defeated retire from the city.

22nd December
German forces blocked
II Corps of the SS must seek a new route towards Liège.

24th December
Allied air power is brought to bear on the Germans
The atrocious weather, which grounded Allied aircraft, allowed the Germans to advance without fear of attack from above, receded. However, the clear skies led to extremely cold nights as well as freezing days.

26th December
British and American forces halt the German advance
The 29th Armoured Brigade and the 2nd Armoured Division check the German advance before the river Meuse.
Relief forces reach Bastogne
Troops from Third Army reach the encircled soldiers in Bastogne.

27th December
Germans driven back
The British XXX Corps pushes the Germans out of the Belgian village of Celles.

31st December
XXX Corps retake Rochefort
Montgomery moves and prepares this force for the major counterattack.

1st January 1945
Operation *Bodenplatte*
The Luftwaffe, hoping to neutralise Allied airpower, launches its attack on airfields around the Battle of the Bulge.

3rd January
The major counterattack in the north begins
British and American forces begin the counterattack, they achieved good initial success but operations had to be postponed for two days due to dreadful weather. The attack resumed its intensity on

5th January
The aim was to reach Houffalize.

7th January
The Germans fall back across the northern shoulder of the bulge
American forces supported by British army units retake many Belgian towns. Between 3rd and 7th January the settlements of Bure, Vielsalm, Salmchâteau, and Grimbiermont, as well as strategically important road links were reached.
The infamous press conference
Montgomery holds his press conference and inadvertently angers many of his American partners.

10th January
La Roche liberated
British forces retake the town of La-Roche-en-Ardenne.

11th January
Saint-Hubert liberated
The 6th Airborne Division reach Saint-Hubert, thus connecting with the left flank of Third Army.

16th January
Allied armies link up
First Army and Third Army link up at Houffalize and then move eastwards to finally eliminate the bulge.

28th January
The Battle of the Bulge has ended in total failure
The totality of the territory captured by the Germans during the Battle of the Bulge was now retaken by the allies.

About the Author

THE AUTHOR, ROBERT Oulds M.A., has a keen interest in military affairs, politics and history. As matters relating to military operations are often closely intertwined with politics, the author's involvement with both national and transnational affairs gives him a good grounding in international relations. And it gives him a useful understanding of the wider strategic significance of major questions regarding Britain's involvement in the world.

Robert Oulds is the longstanding Director of the Bruges Group, the respected think tank which for more than three decades has been at the forefront of the debate about the UK's relationship with the wider world. Their research, which informs both members of the press and politics, is often reported in the media. Robert Oulds regularly appears on the television and the radio debating topical issues. The President of the Bruges Group was the former Prime Minister the late Baroness Margaret Thatcher. As such he is very familiar with the public policy process.

His meticulous research skills have also been honed by his authorship of a great deal of material on many political and international issues, and this gives him the skill of making complex strategic issues accessible to the general public. This allows him to uncover for the first time the full story behind Montgomery and the Battle of the Bulge.

Robert Oulds is the author of *Everything You Wanted To Know About the EU, But Were Afraid to* Ask, and *Montgomery and the First War on Terror*. This book details another little known period of Monty's career. Bernard Law Montgomery, later Field Marshal Viscount Montgomery of Alamein, faced guerrilla forces in Ireland in the early 1920s and Palestine on the eve of the Second World War. This book explores the lessons of Monty's victories in those conflicts and how they should be applied today in the modern war on terror.

Since 2002 the author has also served his community as a local government Councillor in a London Borough. This led him to become a Chairman of Planning and the Cabinet Member with responsibility for Education and Children's Services. His involvement in politics also led to him becoming a chairman of two Parliamentary Constituency Associations.

Robert Oulds actively recognises the deep debt of gratitude which we owe in this country to our armed forces. As such he was Standard Bearer and Treasurer for his local branch of the Royal British Legion (RBL). This is an organisation established to help the welfare of ex-Servicemen and its campaign on issues relating to the armed forces. The RBL are also the custodians of the nation's Remembrance services; and they organise and run the annual Poppy Appeal which raises funds for the aid of our soldiers, sailors, airmen, and women as well as their dependents. The author is impressed by the efforts taken by Montgomery to ensure the safety of his soldiers.

Robert Oulds' Grandfather served as a soldier under the main protagonist in this book, Bernard Law Montgomery, in North Africa, Sicily, Italy, and at Arnhem during the Second World War.

Endnotes

1 Eisenhower, Dwight D, *Crusade in Europe*, William Heinemann Ltd, pages 370 – 373
2 Farrington, Karen, *Witness to World War II*, Abbeydale Press, page 224
3 Reynolds, Michael, *Monty and Patton: Two Paths to Victory*, Spellmount, page 262
4 Eisenhower, Dwight D, *Crusade in Europe*, William Heinemann Ltd, pages 382 – 383
5 Zaloga, Stephen J, *Battles of World War II: Battle of the Bulge 1944 (1) Osprey*, page 90
6 Reynolds, Michael, *Monty and Patton: Two Paths to Victory*, Spellmount, page 264
7 Wilmot, Chester, *The Struggle for Europe*, Wordsworth, 1952, page 611
8 Montgomery, Bernard Law, *The Memoirs of Field-Marshal Montgomery*, Collins, 1958
9 Eisenhower, Dwight D, *Crusade in Europe*, William Heinemann Ltd, page 389
10 Reynolds, Michael, *Monty and Patton: Two Paths to Victory*, Spellmount, pages 268 - 270
11 Eisenhower, Dwight D, *Crusade in Europe*, William Heinemann Ltd, page 398
12 Montgomery, Bernard Law, *A History of Warfare*, Collins, page 527
13 Field Marshal Montgomery, *Normandy to the Baltic*, British Army of the Rhine Stationary Service, 1946
14 Eisenhower, Dwight D, *Crusade in Europe*, William Heinemann Ltd

www.ingramcontent.com/pod-product-compliance
Lightning Source LLC
Chambersburg PA
CBHW030311100526
44590CB00012B/596